Speed Enforced by Aircraft

OTHER BOOKS BY RICHARD PEABODY

Blue Suburban Skies (forthcoming, Main Street Rag Press, 2012)
Last of the Red Hot Magnetos (Paycock Press, 2004)
Sugar Mountain (Argonne House Press, 2000)
Mood Vertigo (Argonne House Press, 1999)
Open Joints on Bridge (Argonne House Press, 1999)
Buoyancy and Other Myths (Gut Punch Press, 1995)
Sad Fashions (Gut Punch Press, 1990)
Paraffin Days (Cumberland Press, 1985)
Echt & Ersatz (Paycock Press, 1985)
I'm in Love with the Morton Salt Girl (Paycock Press, 1979)

BOOKS EDITED BY RICHARD PEABODY

Amazing Graces:Yet Another Collection of Fiction by Washington Area Women
    (Paycock Press, 2012)
Gravity Dancers: Even More Fiction by Washington Area Women
    (Paycock Press, 2009)
Stress City:A Big Book of Fiction by 51 DC Guys (Paycock Press, 2008)
Electric Grace: Still More Fiction by Washington Area Women (Paycock Press,
    2007)
Kiss the Sky: Fiction and Poetry Starring Jimi Hendrix (Paycock Press, 2007)
Enhanced Gravity: More Fiction by Washington Area Women (Paycock Press,
    2006)
Sex & Chocolate:Tasty Morsels for Mind and Body, w/Lucinda Ebersole
    (Paycock Press, 2006)
Conversations with Gore Vidal, w/Lucinda Ebersole (Univ. of Mississippi Press,
    2005)
Alice Redux: New Stories of Alice, Lewis, and Wonderland (Paycock Press, 2005)
31 Arlington Poets, Spoken Word CD (Paycock Press, 2004)
In Praise of What Persists, a posthumous collection of short stories by Joyce Ren-
    wick, (Paycock Press, 2004)
Grace and Gravity: Fiction by Washington Area Women (Paycock Press, 2004)
A Different Beat:Writing by Women of the Beat Generation
    (Serpent's Tail/High Risk, 1997)
Mondo James Dean, w/Lucinda Ebersole (St. Martin's Press, 1996)
Loose Change,A posthumous book of unpublished poetry and prose by the late
    British Poet Tina Fulker, (Bogg Publications, 1995)
Mondo Marilyn, w/Lucinda Ebersole (St. Martin's Press, 1995)
Coming to Terms:A Literary Response to Abortion, w/Lucinda Ebersole
    (The New Press, 1995)
Mondo Elvis, w/ Lucinda Ebersole (St. Martin's Press, 1994)
Mondo Barbie, w/ Lucinda Ebersole (St. Martin's Press, 1993)
Mavericks: nine independent publishers (Paycock Press, 1983)
DC Magazines:A Literary Retrospective (Paycock Press, 1981)

Speed Enforced by Aircraft

Richard Peabody

BRP
Broadkill River Press

Acknowledgements

Some of these poems have appeared in print or online or are forthcoming in:
Abbey, Bareback, Blind Oracle, Dead Mule School of Literature, Delmarva Review, Frantic Egg, Iodine, Kenning, Lines + Stars, Loch Raven Review, Main Street Rag, Manila Envelope, Milk Sugar, Minimus, MIPOesias, MIPO Companion, Mission at Tenth, Muddy River Poetry Review, Our Day's Encounter, Paterson Literary Review, Petrichor Review, Phantom Kangaroo, Platte Valley Review, Poet Lore, Red Booth Review, riverbabble, Shady Side Review, Solo Café, Thrush Poetry, Tiferet Journal, Tin Lustre Mobile, Whiskey Island Review, and *Wordwrights!*

Others appear in the anthologies:
Babylon Burning: 9/11 five years on, ed. Todd Swift, (nthposition, London, England, 2006)
DC Poets Against the War, ed. by Sarah Browning, Michele Elliott & Danny Rose (Argonne House Press, 2004)
No Place Like Here: An Anthology of Southern Delaware Poetry & Prose, ed. by Billie Travalini (doll's eye press, 2011)
Poems for Lord Hutton, ed. by Todd Swift (nthposition, London, England, 2003)
Poetic Voices without Borders, ed. by Robert Giron (Gival Press, 2005)
Short Fuse: The Global Anthology of New Fusion Poetry, ed. by Todd Swift and Philip Norton (Ratapallax Press, 2002)
Times New Roman: Poets Oppose 21st Century Empire, ed. by Todd Swift, (Nthposition, London, England, 2003)

Two poems previously appeared in my Ebook *Rainflowers* (ahadada press, 2002)

Original author photo by Margaret Grosh
Typesetting by Barbara Shaw

LOC Control Number: 2012941557
ISBN: 978-0-9826030-6-2

BRP
Broadkill River Press

James C.L. Brown, Publisher
Broadkill River Press
104 Federal Street,
Milton, Delaware 19968
E-mail: the_broadkill_press@earthlink.net

"There are so many little dyings every day, it doesn't matter which one of them is death."

—Kenneth Patchen

For Twyla and Laurel
my dear hearts

I want to thank Jamie Brown and Sid Gold for gathering all of this together and seeing it through to book-in-hand. I also need to thank a lotta folks who have helped me out this past decade— Shane Allison, Ron Baker, Kevin & Lili Bezner, Eugenie Bisulco, Nicole Blackman, Sarah Browning, Grace Cavalieri, Vikram Chandra, Gary Clift, Jennifer Dante, Suzanne Delgaetano, Deanna D'errico, Ram Devineni, M. Scott Douglass, Blair Ewing, Bernadette Geyer, Robert L. Giron, Jesse Glass, Dan Johnson, Amy King, Janna Kollias, Karen J. Kovacs, M.L. Liebler, Didi Menendez, Diane Meredith, Miles David Moore, Terence Mulligan, Phil Norton, W.T. Pfefferle, Kim Roberts, Irene Rouse, Martha Sanchez-Lowery, Daniel Sendecki, Rose Solari, Todd Swift, Henry Taylor, Cheryl Townsend, Chris Walsh, Susan Weinberg, and Sharlie West. And lastly—lots of love to everybody at Blue Mountain Center and The Virginia Center for the Creative Arts for putting me up and putting up with me.

CONTENTS

IV

V

VI

VII

VIII

I

Reston Zoo, 2004

Two-year-old Laurel asks to go "Uppy"
so I lift her onto my left shoulder.
I walk her around the Canada Geese
who moments ago knocked her cup of seed
from her hand and scared her with
incredibly loud honking.

Aggressive birds easily twice her size.
It's hot. A July day that just won't quit.
No shade. Our petting zoo picnic rushed
so we can take the tractor ride. See the llamas,
the zebra. At least that's how I remember it.

Hot, sweaty, restless, and so when I spot
a set of steps near a penned area
I automatically climb them
with sun-burned Laurel in my arms.

The pen appears to be empty.
It takes a minute to spot them.
Alligators. Two of them.
Maybe 4' long? 5' max.
It's broiling but they have
a little shade and a pond
to slither in and out of.

And they just sit there like logs.
"Alligators," I say. And I point
like men always do. "Look."
And Laurel imitates me. Pointing.
She says something in her too loud
outdoor voice and the closest
alligator's eyes open. "Look," I say,
"he's awake." And he's moving.

Moving closer. And closer.
Faster than I've ever seen a large reptile
move. Until he's immediately below
where I hold Laurel. No bars. No roof.
Just a daddy holding his daughter in his
arms within plain view of a predator.

The alligator waits. Unhinges its jaws.
No, I must be imagining things.
I back down the stairs. The walls of their
grassy pen as high as my chest. I watch
the alligator as I circle the pen. He follows us.
Laurel is laughing. I climb another set
of stairs. Now the second Alligator rushes
over. This one startles me with a loud hiss.

I finally understand—they think it's feeding time.
They think I'm going to drop my baby into the pen.
I squeeze Laurel tight to my chest. She's scared
of the hissing. Aware of my fear now.
She's started fussing. She wants mommy.

We hustle back down the stairs to my wife and
my older daughter. But I am shaken.
I have brushed up against something dank and dark
and primeval. An alien mind where humans are meat.

I want my mommy, too. I want somebody to step in
to protect me in a dangerous world where I'm not
adequate enough to protect my daughter, or myself.

Maraschino Cherries

Red attracts children.
And then you're hooked.

As a kid you never get enough of them
unless your mother likes fruity drinks.

Finally ate my fill
when I worked in a bar.

All that red dye.

Like eating the heart of
a candy animal.

El Santuario de Chimayo

A little blind girl in a yellow calico dress
is walking hand-in-hand with her Papi
down the hill to the pink and sandstone
tinted sanctuary of miracle healing.

She wears a black bandana about her eyes
studded with silver *milagros*. She wears
shiny Mary Jane's. Her Papi is whispering
to her. His tone solemn, reverential.

Inside the Catholic church they pass
the brutalized *santero* of Christ.
Homage to the Penitentes?
The flagellant sect that lead a
procession during Holy Week.
The pair light votives.
They cross themselves with water,
then kneel and pray before
a crayon-colored altar.

In time they join other pilgrims
at *El Pocito* (the little well)
to dig into the sacred pit of healing dirt.
A sign reads, "Please This Earth Is Blessed.
Do Not Play In It. Thank You."
The girl let's go of her Papi's hand and
plunges an index finger into the fragrant circle.

Before her Papi can bend down,
distracted by the Prayer Room

filled with crutches, braces and naïve art,
she grabs two fistfuls of burnt red dirt
and in one swift motion
raises her black *milagros* covered bandana
and shoves both hands into her eyes.

Her Papi catches her as she licks each finger,
the grit between her teeth, falling from her cheeks.
She smiles, saying, "*Papi Papi, que buen gusto.*"

Tiny Black Coffin
(Adirondack Museum, NY)

I'm eager to see the spoils of the Gilded Age—
a private railroad car, stagecoaches, a cariole.

America's Castles:Adirondack Camps plays
on video screens scattered through the buildings.

My eyes drink in everything. There's a racing sloop,
a complete blacksmith's shop, and a carpentry display.

That's where I freeze—in front of a tiny black coffin.
Big enough only for an infant or a toddler.

No denying life was hard here for the locals
though this seems out of synch with the Hands-On

displays, "Kid's Corner," and impressive playground.
My girls would no doubt be bored if I dragged

them into this museum. We'd have to play and
hit the café. Climb the steps of the Fire Tower.

They'd speed right past this box without even
seeing it, without realizing its purpose.

I'm 200 feet above one of the most beautiful panoramas—
Blue Mountain Lake as the autumn leaves begin to change.

And here's this tiny black box. And I think back
to the birth of my first child and the 24-hour labor.

My joy and stark realization after the Caesarian
that a hundred years ago I would have lost them both.

Wife and daughter. And so, a tiny black coffin,
too insignificant to contain the immensity of such

a loss. Too awful to contemplate fully. The weight,
the terrible weight of that death. So, ignoring the

Do Not Touch signs, and knowing they'll throw me
out of the place, I do the only thing I know—

I pull the tiny black coffin from the wall. Hug it to
my chest as I would my daughters. And then I rock

the rough-hewn box back and forth, back and forth,
aware that nothing can compensate for such pain.

Empire Building

Put down the stick.
Put it down.
You could poke out an eye.

Because Daddy said.
Put it down.

Do you want a time out?
No? Then put down the stick.

Because Daddy said so.

No rocks.
Take that out of your mouth.
Give it to me.
Give it to me. Right now.

Okay, you're through.
Time out.
Now just sit in that chair.

Stay there.
I told you to stay put.
I'm sorry you're crying.
But that's too bad.
Now sit.

Because you might hurt somebody.
That's why. You might hurt yourself.

Now put that down.
Stop it.
I told you to stop it. Right now.

Okay, give me the oil.
Give it to me.
Because I said so.
Because you're not old enough
to use that yet.

Daddy spank.
I mean it Daddy spank.

Nuages

(after Django Reinhardt)

1

She's lost amidst her sleeping cubs
like otters in a nature film.

One girl horizontal across the bed
the other vertical with her hair
fanned along my wife's stomach.

How does she sleep?

Buttery moonlight spotlights skin.
Softens everything.

I watch from the doorway.

Earlier they were like tiny animals—
fighting sleep. Melting down.

"Read me another story."

So how did I become a boring old fart
who writes poems like this one?

And yet there's power
in this jumble of bodies,

in this simultaneous
breathing,

and I don't wish
to disturb

this magic wife,
this family
that doesn't appear

to need me at all.

2

My wife has flown to Brazil
so I'm in bed
curved around my daughters.

Impossible to sleep.
I listen for every breath.

One holds my hand
in dreamy dreams and the other
flops like a salmon and kicks
a leg over mine.

Our birds never seem to sleep either,
songs drifting upstairs
from trees below.

The world is coming to an end
they sing.

The sky is falling.

I lie awake in bed
clinging to my daughters,
my life raft,

painting them a bright future,

painting them any future
I can manage.

The banana moon
through the skylight.

Songs drifting
drifting

Bossa Nova

blue

tide.

Winchester Model '94/Pre 1964

When my father died I kept one of his rifles.
A Winchester repeating rifle just like the ones
I saw in TV westerns when I was growing up.

I'd fired this particular gun as a teenager at
makeshift rifle ranges with my father. And I
loved the gold gleam of the metal against the dark

lubricated wood. It was light and felt good
nestled into my shoulder and didn't have
too much of a kick. Not that I remember anyway.

I hadn't fired it in more than a decade since his death.
Though I still had a box of shells. So when my wife
was pregnant with our first child I decided that

I didn't want the rifle around the house any longer.
We called the Arlington police and turned in the gun.
Which would have been the end of it except that the

young officer fell in love with the rifle, too.
"I can't take this. You know they just destroy guns
that are turned in," he said. He was belligerent

and hurt at the same time. He didn't see how a man
could throw away something as marvelous as a Winchester '94.
But his carrying on reminded me of the bad things

about my father that always piss me off. So I was adamant.
"We're having a baby, and we don't want the gun in the house.
My wife and I have agreed and that's what we want."

"Tell you what," he said. "You keep the rifle for an hour
and I'll drive straight home and get one of my rifles and we'll
swap. And I'll turn that one in and keep this one."

I looked at him like he was completely out of his mind.
He shook his head and realized how preposterous this sounded.
"No, it just won't work. What a shame. A damn shame," he said.

And we watched as he marched off the porch to his patrol car.
He sighted down the rifle at an imaginary jackrabbit, worked
the action like a gunfighter, and then popped the trunk and

put down the gun. Who knows what finally happened?
Maybe he turned it in for disposal. Maybe he quit the force
to roam the dusty red mesas of Monument Valley? Who can say?

The Winchester '94 was a classic no doubt. Maybe I should have
sold it to an antique gun specialist? I don't have regrets—though
there are times I get nostalgic for that primitive shape on my wall.

Baby Snot on My Shirt at Whole Foods

Did I really lust after
these unnaturally thin blondes

Dressed head to toe in black

Their small dark hearts
and insect-like cell phones

Who furtively glance at me

Baby on board my back
like I'm a plague carrier.

I Find Myself at Gymboree
With Holes in Both Socks

Shoes come off at the door
so I can tread mats like some gymnast.

I'm new at this and my daughter is cranky.
Class has started. I'm the only father.

Two holes. And the Yuppie wives
from Fairfax with their perfect teeth
and SUVs say nothing.

I wish I were French
or at least Brazilian,
wearing cool shades,
vaguely dangerous.

But I feel small.

The Incredible Shrinking Man
my new idol.

II

Holding Pattern

You have always taken great comfort
in the planes circling high above the runway.

Older now, the air traffic has slowed somewhat
but even a wife and family hasn't altered some
flights or flight paths.

You allow this, one girlfriend told you, in a major
argument about retroactive lovers and nebulous
possibilities.

Women understand that flirtation is an art form
by the time they're three years old. You have witnessed
this close-up. You are supposed to shut them down,
to cancel the flight, flash the ring. But this often
seems detrimental to your so-called career.

In a field where availability is frequently a key
to publication, scholarships, grants, and positions
it helps to be a melancholy poet of possibility.

Nobody ever admits this in print. But in private
many joke about the woman at the writer's colony—
was it Yaddo or McDowell?—who powdered her nose
with her diaphragm.

Yes, you admit you allow it. You're not Johnny Depp.
Not even close. Even now you marvel that there are any
planes left in the sky. That any pinpoint your runway.

Remember how the P.R. folks hid Cynthia in the early
Beatles blitz? John Lennon was married? With a baby?
Who knew? Secrets can be of use.

The blonde, brunette, redhead airlines continue to pursue
daily flights to your fair city. You're constantly aware of this
if only in the tiny conservatory in the back of your brain.

D.H. Lawrence would understand. Sometimes you gloat.
Frequently you juggle guilt and desire and memory.

The planes circle. You try to ignore their takeoffs and landings.
Yet point out an airplane in the sky. "Look airplane," you
say to your 2-year-old. She claps. Repeats, "Airplane."
"Bye bye airplane," you say. "Bye bye."

You will always keep watching the skies.

My Cheating Heart

My wife wants an apology.
Apparently I cheated on her in a dream.
I try to laugh it off. Sleepy. Hugging my pillow.
She won't have any of that. She says, "I mean it.
Apologize. Right now." I keep laughing.

I compare notes with friends throughout the day.
Worried that my wife is cracking up. She's been under a
lot of stress lately. I mean dreams aren't real . . . are they?
My buddies laugh, too. Partly at the situation and partly
at my sorry ass. The gals all say the same thing—"Apologize."
"But I didn't do anything wrong!" I protest. They're not
buying it either. Dreams seem to be the new turf where
the gender wars are being fought.

I eat lunch and sulk. It's ridiculous. My wife is acting crazy.
One woman asks me whom I was sleeping with? "What?" "In your
        dream."
"It wasn't my dream, it was her dream." "So whom were you sleeping
        with?"
"I don't know. Some blonde." "Mister, you have got to apologize."
"No way," I said. "Never." She just shook her head. "Have it your way."

My wife won't talk to me when she gets home. I've been banished to
        the basement.
All because I had imaginary sex with a figment of her imagination.
        She won't tell me
if it's anybody she knows. Could be an actress or a Super Model.
        I have no idea.
Yet I stand accused. Guilty with no chance of parole.

I finally give up. The basement's cold. I can't get over how stupid
all of this is. And when I apologize, "for having imaginary sex in your
        dream
last night," my wife starts crying. I move to hold her and she smacks
        my arm,

Pushes me away. "You're just making fun of me," she says. "You don't
     really mean it."

And so I try to sleep beside my wife as she sobs. My brain playing a
     slide show of
every blonde I have ever seen in my entire life. Picturing one fantasy
     sequence
after another, so that at least my punishment fits my imaginary crime.

When She Walked in the Room

Not as smart as the rest.
Not beautiful yet at ease
in a way none of the other students
have achieved.

Arriving late.

A mean girl
comfortable with her body.

Sitting with legs open
panties on view to the world.

She flashed cleavage when she leaned over.
Had to be reminded about today's assignment.

Flashing flesh and a whiff of eroticism
as though she were in control of the entire class.

I'm a married man with two wonderful kids
and I no longer lust after teenagers

but her legs draw my eyes
over and over again. And she knows it.

They also draw the eyes of the woman
who'd invited me to lecture on poetry.

Afterwards we are both astonished
that no matter what we did we were drawn

again and again to glance between this
blond woman's legs.

Ashamed of the control
she had over both of us.

Unable to comprehend how such a thing
is possible in one so young.

Angry at being so blatantly toyed with
when so many other women in the class

were so brilliant and creative.
And yet hours later it's the one who

stooped to sexual grandstanding that I recall.
The one who troubles my sleep.

The one I couldn't look in the eye.

Friday Night [No] Lights

We drove aimlessly in the Autumn dusk
looking for a place to make love in our town.

You chose the fifty-yard line of your high school.
Some issues to work out even though you'd graduated.

October's fingers sent a chill down my neck
or was it your fingers, settling me down.

How could you be so calm? Me always paranoid.
Afraid we'd get in trouble.

You pulled your corduroys down. Boy pants.
I was still adjusting to the fact that you never wore underwear.

The lime from the football field sticking
to your arms, your back, your hair.

Lola gets whatever Lola wants.
Working some internal magic

draining us both expertly
rolling me onto my back

down the midfield stripe.
I'd look like a skunk the rest of the night.

Resting my head against your breasts
as I shake and quake

my heart ready to catapult
from my chest.

Honeysuckle at Night

I fake sleep
while you strip

toss clothes
onto pine floor.

Do you always do that
when I'm not around?

Just clean up for me?
Your neatness fetish a big act.

Or is it my influence
this new sloppiness?

Full moon light
kissing your feet.

You walking
on ivory tiptoes

Trysting
(Dumbarton Oaks, Washington, DC)

skinny dipping
in the midst of power ties
and haute couture

I should come back in the daylight
view the relics

half-glimpsed
Byzantine moon

the word "Loggia" turns me on

Lest I forget:
damask skin
intimacy

luscious pool

III

Green-Eyed Monsters

Jealousy and bitterness are the bread and butter
of many talented writers.

When my students succeed I'm ecstatic.
I celebrate with them and for them.

But when their success eclipses my own,
when they get the big $ gigs,

land on talk shows and secure the
grants and multiple book contracts,

I get a little green around the gills
like an Iguana on steroids.

And when they ask me what to do
with their first six figure pay check,

and are surprised when I say
I've never had one,

it's as though we both hear a click—
a door closing, a chasm separating us,

the teacher and the writer,
the wannabe and the real thing.

At times like those I can hear Elvis
singing "It's now or never."

And I reach for a bigger knife
so I can spread my bitterness

and jealousy
more evenly

Blue Mountain Center

The bicycle slides on the sandy downhill
as I try to dismount like a rodeo cowboy
only to crash in a pratfall of epic proportions.

I'm on my back and laughing. Embarrassed.
I look like an idiot. A turtle upside down
kicking legs in the air. Poets are ridiculous.

Admitting Defeat

Eels have made a mess of my net again,
moving needles through a stitch.

I scream like a three-month-old
whose mother has gone back to work.

Grasp the hideous mouth
and pry the slimy thing apart.

The imagination flees,
racing away with the clouds,
with the rain,

leaving me
alone and bleak,

wishing I could
get through this net of language,

balanced on my tongue
like a warm sip

of imported beer.

Library Book Sale

Late March 2001 and it's gray and rainy.
Naturally I've come without a coat or hat
to discover the sale is in the parking garage.

I shiver through fiction and literature,
eavesdrop on a couple of young poets
namedropping Rosmarie Waldrop,

and slide into their space to check
out the poetry section. And it's all here.
Every poet who mattered in the 70s and 80s.

Norman Dubie, Cynthia Macdonald, David
St. John, Stephen Dunn, Albert Goldbarth,
Marilyn Hacker, James Tate, Tess Gallagher, and more.

And none of these volumes have been checked out—
not one single one of them by any of these
name poets—since as far back as 1986.

Which is why the library has stamped WITHDRAWN
on their jackets, and why the books are piled high
on the Sale heap, priced at a dollar or 50 cents.

Every last one of these mid-career poets
thinking someday they'd be the next Eliot or Pound
or Doc Williams, every last one teaching someplace

right now. And I shiver and pass them over
in favor of Neruda, and Heine, and D. H. Lawrence.

IV

Civil War Pieta

Dear Walt:

Did you ever embrace feet? The absence of feet?
Hold poor wounded feet captive in your hands. Caress them.
Ankles, instep, foot-ball, toes, toe-joints, the heel.
Attempt to mold the damaged clay of muscle and bone
until it once again resembled the perfect feet of newborns.
My dancer girlfriend had the most desirable legs imaginable.
Yet I cried when she stripped off her shoes and I saw
that she only possessed three remaining toenails.
She couldn't paint them like my daughters do now.
Couldn't wear open toed shoes. Once she painted
my nails bloody red. Not like the brownish real blood
you saw daily at Armory Square Hospital
on your rounds from cot to cot. Tears in your beard.
Tears falling onto mangled sinew, the pale flesh of those
bravehearted boys. Good brave boys, many of them
doomed amputees. My relationships with dancers
were always doomed for less dynamic reasons.
Bloody scabs woven into pink silk ballet slippers. Stripping off
her pointe shoes thread by thread after she danced to reveal
her torn pitiful feet. I'm not a foot fetishist but a woman's feet
are extremely appealing, glorious, mystical.
A curve, an arch, a flexing of toes, a rocking of legs.
Bathing a soldier's feet, did you think analogous thoughts?
Give me to bathe the memories of all dead soldiers.
Did you wish you could heal them with a laying on of hands?
Long for some of the expensive perfume that sinner woman used
on the savior's feet? *Perfume therefore my chant, O love!*
immortal Love! Did you dream that by soothing these
men, by handling their wounded, ravaged flesh, their
stumps, their broken, savaged, gangrenous toes,
you could somehow make them whole once more? Free them?
Feet of war, feet of warriors, feet that nobody would ever kiss
or even touch again. Did you think why then I shall kiss them.

39

And parted the shirt from my bosom-bone, and plunged
your tongue to my bare-stript heart.
I shall touch them—these wounds, these wounded. Blue or gray
no longer an issue in a landscape fraught with cannon fire, pestilence,
and death. Nothing mattering but pain, and new worlds of pain,
combined with a hunger to capture a new reality via your
brain and heart, your tears. Did you stoop then, heft the boy
up into your arms in search of breath? Curl your body around his sad form?
Hospital linens draping you both, freezing you momentarily.
Sweet are the blooming cheeks of the living!
Before you rocked gently, gently like a tired ship on an ocean of tears.

Mathew Brady

Another rags-to-riches-to-rags story
for one of Washington's Native Sons.

Brady opened a show called,
"The Dead of Antietam" in 1862

shocking audiences with stills
of corpse after bloated corpse.

The first time the American public
witnessed war's horror and reality.

Turns out though he's credited for
most photos from the Civil War era

the bulk were taken by his intrepid staff
or else purchased at a much later date

to become part of his massive collection.

Brady bet everything on his Civil War photos
only to have the public turn a blind eye

not very long after Appomattox.
America didn't want to remember.

Mathew Brady died broke, in debt,
almost entirely forgotten.

Military Fantasia

War Movies never get it right.
The audience would never stomach the truth.

At Agincourt
the outnumbered English soldiers
were surrounded by bodies of the fallen
to a height of 18 deep.

Imagine.

They climbed atop the piles
and continued to bludgeon
and swing their swords and axes
at the demoralized French cavalry.

Antietam.
Bloody Lane.
The first four lines of
Confederate infantry
simply vanished in the grapeshot.

At Verdun
the pigs consumed
the dying and the dead.

Pigs will eat anything
including their young.

Private Ryan is praised for accuracy
yet most soldiers were killed by
the bones of their blown apart buddies
piercing their skin as shrapnel.
Jaw bones, arms, feet,
fragments.

Omaha Beach
bloodier than Hollywood
could ever hope to imagine.

And still we find ways
to send our children to war.

Those who live by the sword
die by the sword.
And that's too good for them.

Those who don't live by the sword
also die by the sword,
too frequently for my liking.

Photo Realism

Were the Khmer Rouge barbarous children?
Or demons made flesh?

Their infatuation with cameras
with certifying every single death
as baffling

as the soldiers at Abu Ghraib
using their cell phones

to record the horror
they thought comic.

Americans don't like the comparison
as though there are gradations of evil.

The image of that hooded prisoner
as immortal as any photos

Mathew Brady took of the dead
confederates at Bloody Lane
after the Battle of Antietam,

or the slaughtered innocents
at Kent State or My Lai.

Demons walk the earth
and cloak their actions
with words like: Righteousness,
Security, Honor, Freedom.

The mind is a camera
and we remember.

Couch Commandos

have a board game mentality
in a GameBoy world.

Closest they've ever come to real action
was playing Stratego back in the day.

They wouldn't know Kuma/War
from *Combat* starring Vic Morrow.

Yet if you ask them
they will bury you in stats
about Hummers, depleted uranium rounds,
body armor, and high tech weaponry.

Couch commandos worship
at the Tom Clancy tabernacle.

Though John Wayne has always
been closer to their ideal.

White men love hardware so much
they have no room whatsoever
for the complicated software of the heart.

Ask them how many Iraqi women and children
have died during two Gulf wars?

Go ahead ask them.

Iraqi Freedom? Who cares!

Funny how their rationales always vanish
when things start to get a little real.

The Iraqi people have never entered
into any of their military scenarios.

Iraqi people aren't sexy enough
for the Couch Commandos

who punch *Sexy Girls Sexy Guns*
back into their DVD players and drift

downstream to a time before celluloid heroes
when real men still walked the earth.

The Untimely Death

"When I hear the word Security, I reach for my shotgun."
                                        - Robyn Hitchcock

I am rescuing the dead
dipping deep into their sleep
returning them whole in dreams

Dreams of revenge
truth
freedom

When good men die
from painkillers and slit wrists
the punishing kiss

and liars propagate
I think 007
and Eton Rifles

THEY will stop at nothing
to silence truth
to spin their lies

I am rescuing the dead
from the Haruspex
from the spies

from the world leaders
who believe blood is truth
my country right or wrong

I am rescuing the dead

The Bones of Patroclus

Nobody knows where you end
and I begin

bones mingled in a grave.

I didn't want you
as much as I wanted to be you.

Younger, stronger,
blessed by the gods.

Even your shiny armor
more distinctive.

The only way I knew
to get you out of your funk.

To masquerade as Mr. Rage.

I should have kicked your ass.
Though I never could.

Moping about a slave girl
when you had me.

You could be such
a fat-headed moron.

I adored being you
until Hector caught me.

A lapse of judgment.

I thought I was just as tough
that I could take him.

Well, you got your revenge.
And I did force you back into the war

though not the way I intended.

Turns out you weren't immortal after all.
Your mom sure blew that one.

But I've got you now Achilles.
Them bones them bones.

Blended together over time
like the peanut brittle of the gods.

Shootout at the Arlington Arts Center

A lone brother shooting hoops.
Deserted playground. Clang.
B-ball off the rim. Another
clang missed hook shot.
Self-conscious. Ego shrinking.
My little girl clapping cuz she's
so excited to see the slides.
As the big man shooter clangs
an easy lay-up. Keep walking.
I'm the only witness. Like
catching your parents in bed.
Clang. Now he's dribbling,
eyeing me, wishing me gone.
How many shots can anybody
miss when they're six plus feet tall?
Clang. I stop watching. This is
just too incredible. A huge man
who now throws up air ball after air ball.
With nobody defending him except
maybe the bogeyman. Does Mike
ever have a day like this? Even little me
can make a few of these shots. Some
days the blues must put rocks in your shoes.

Trail of Tears
(The American Indian Museum, Washington DC)

The sacred mesa has come
to the white man's capital.

Bringing spirit magic.
Four sacred directions.

Grandfather rocks
from Hudson Bay, Chile,
Hawaii, and Great Falls.

This museum is a time machine
set in motion by prisms.

Ghost dances
Sipapus

Kachinas
Vigas

A Trojan Horse
planted in the checkerboard city
of black and white

where invisible red men
flex their muscles.

A flying saucer landing
in the nest of the blue shirt
and power tie.

"Take me to your leader."

A war cry
in a procession
of broken treaties.

Fire pits
Yellow thunder

Sacred magic
transplanted from earth's womb

elemental limestone chant
harmonic convergence

Visiting the Dead

The first dead bodies I ever saw
were in my father's illustrated
Civil War magazines. Mathew Brady's
photos of Devil's Den at Gettysburg.
Bodies at Gaines' Mill. Bodies at
Malvern Hill. Bodies at Antietam.

Places that were within a few hours
reach of Washington, DC.

Many down the road on Route 29. Known
as [Robert E.] Lee Highway.

We'd cross the Potomac and drive all the way
to my grandmother's in North Carolina.

The first little boy I ever knew lived
in Culpeper. They had a Traffic Fatality
Sign midtown that featured the
Grim Reaper. A spooky rendering
I will never ever forget. Right up there
with the Ghost of Christmas Yet to Come
in Dickens's *Christmas Carol.*

When we visited Gettysburg for the
very first time I was disappointed
because I expected to find the soldiers
still there—frozen in place. And the bodies.

There are no photos of Pickett's Charge.
Only artist's renderings. I guess even Brady
couldn't focus a camera on carnage
of that magnitude.

Savages in Our Underwear

An odor of honeysuckle rotting
by a creek's muddy banks. I can see
the white bridge where I played as a boy.
Vines we swung on.

Cascades of laughter sheltered us
from form and function,
the imposition
of antlers.

Our tickets not yet punched
for the war or oblivion express.

V

Black Rose Day

Cancer is a flower

an inky black rose
boiling in your throat

tangled vines
too watery to touch

rising to the surface
to blossom

a ringing phone
at the end of July

Night School

My father passed on to me what his own father had bequeathed to him—
anger and punishment will mold a boy. The only way to get through
my thick skull was with a switch, or a belt, or the back of a hand.

My father wanted me to beat my dog like he beat me.
Because Beagles bark all of the time and my father wouldn't allow
a dog indoors. Because the neighbors were old and retired and

couldn't get any sleep with my dog barking for companionship.
So, night after endless night I whipped my dog until she bled.
Crying because I was only twelve and she just wouldn't learn.

Crying as she yelped and jumped up from the end of her chain
and licked my face with her devotion and unconditional love.

Box of Soldiers

"Pickup your toys son."

These lost, these fallen.

He drapes the toy box
in his 4th of July flag

13 stars in a circle

The boy hasn't seen
newspaper photos

Not like we did every day
during the Vietnam war

Somehow he intuits
toy box = coffin

Innocence

Unaware that every choice
comes with a loss

a yin-yang you learn
many years later

I'm pretty certain
how the God of the Bible
feels about soldiers

those who choose
to kill for a living.

"Lights out now," I say.
My son puts a single finger to his lips.

"Shh. Daddy, you'll wake them."

"Are they sleeping? Like you should be."

He laughs.
"Silly Daddy, they're dead,
like you should be."

After he falls asleep
I'm down in the basement

unzipping body bags
to find broken toys,
lost causes.

My draft lottery number 12
echoing in my dreams.

Planet Drum

My friend's heart
is beating too fast.

She has always been known
for possessing a good heart.

A wise heart.

A mischievous heart.

I am sad
knowing she is ill.

Her heart opting
for occasional rhythms
over a conventional pulse.

My friend
has never been
conventional.

Even fear
cannot diminish
the heart that beats
within her heart,

a backbeat
strong and true.

Outgrowing My Father

I took my father deep into the rainforest
where the albino python falls
from impossibly tall trees.
They were not convinced he
was snaky enough for them.

I took my father to the mountains
thinking surely he would fit among
the redbuds and mountain laurel.
Wasn't he curmudgeonly enough
to be a bear? But the bears said no.

I took my father to the veldt
thinking surely the lions would love him,
he was born under the sign of Leo after all.
And indeed, the pride liked him, but the
alpha males perceived a threat, and said no.

I took my father up into the sky
thinking surely he would soar. I set him free
above a mountain ridge along the Hudson River.
Hawks and crows mocked him as he fell.
I caught my father before he hit the water.

I took my father out to sea
thinking he's fish then, if nobody else will have him,
Not playful enough for the dolphins,
nor a fast enough swimmer for the bait fish.
The sharks wanted to eat him.
Even the Coelacanth said no.

I took my father home with me
"I'm disappointed," I said. "You've shrunk so much.
Look how small you are now compared to me."
Then placed him beside his father and his
father's father on my ancient history shelf.

Hillbilly Music

A skinny man is reading poems.
Rush hour radio serenading the alley.
A little Hank Williams in the night.

My father appears at the doorway.
His angry heart no longer able
to cry, cheat, or eat gumbo.

I don't believe in ghosts.
So maybe he's really stopping by
having developed a taste for poetry

in the afterlife.
Not that I can hear many words
seated this far back in the gallery.

The skinny poet reads slower than
most children do when learning how.
So what to make of my charismatic father

as he mouths silent words at me.
The fractured English of the poet
at the podium, Hank Williams' yodel,

fusing together on the first warm spring night,
thirteen years after my father's fatal heart attack.
Here I am now in Arlington just a few blocks

from the first apartment he lived in
with my mother and their brand new baby boy
born 50 years and a couple weeks ago.

What to make of silence and coincidence.
As Hank honkytonks into the night sky
and the spaces between the skinny poet's words

get more and more lonesome and blue.

Nostalgia for the Middle Class

What makes a life?

A tattered baseball

A ticket to a show

Pine needles, shoelaces,

The yellowed globe.

Great Dane with a tennis ball

Photographs

Icicles

Or snow

Stalactites

Broken window glass

Bouquet of red and yellow leaves

Bruised apples

A small plane overhead

The memory of words left unsaid.

VI

Yuletide Blues

Group of Freshmen sitting around a table
shooting the shit about the impending holidays.

Lots of privileged I'm going to do this
or that, and go here or there.
Go skiing. Go to the movies. Fly to Aspen,
or LA, or Boulder, or Pasadena.
Eat goose. Eat turkey. Eat venison.
And lots and lots of pie—pecan,
pumpkin and mince-meat.

Damn this is going to be the absolute best.
One guy silent. "What are you gonna do
over the holidays?" And then quietly
so nobody says a word—"I'm going to
go home and work in the coal mine."

I Get Yelled at By Lawyers

Twice in my life.

Always at dawn.
Always about literature.

Once because I dared
ask Katherine Anne Porter
for an interview.

Twice because I tried to
publish a story with parody
Elvis lyrics.

Both times dreaming alone
of my unrequited love.

So close, yet so far.

Let that be a warning
I find myself thinking,

Lawyers and literature
something wicked,

like unrequited love
and John Grisham.

I Get Yelled at By Sterling A. Brown

Because I was young and clueless

Because I tried to corral him for a project

Because his wife died
a few days before my call

Because how was I to know?
And no matter how I backtracked

I was pushing too hard

Because I hadn't learned that real life
trumps literature over and over again

Until now

When I have buried so many people
that I am beginning to understand

What keening sounds like

The difference between a
dog and its bark.

Beauty Always Makes Me Sad

Longing is about
union with something larger.

Perfect innocence.

I'm not talking
desire,
or possession.

People often make that mistake.

More like a series
of overlaid transparencies.

And we,
every one of us,

wants to be rippled
above the template.

Very few
fit into that purity

without
additional illustrations.

And each time
we behold real beauty

we remember.

The Torturer's Apprentice

Forget everything you know about being human
save for anatomy.

Rely on childhood memories
of injuring small animals.

If it can hurt you
it will hurt them.

If you're squeamish
wear earplugs.

Sunglasses
mute the blood.

Take it
one step at a time.

Don't allow anticipation
to ruin your moment.

They always confess.
There's never any doubt.

Yet for you it must be
about the journey.

Torture Splinter #1

Tar and feathers seem
comic until you add
the missing ingredient—
fire.

Torture Splinter #2

How long can a man
live in a box
the size of a coffin?

Peace in Mississippi #1

There are white men living
in Mississippi today

and sometimes I think
that's the entire problem.

Girls with Antlers

You're not used to seeing girls with antlers
shining whitely from their brows
but you have to admit it turns you on.

"Where have you been?" they say.
"It's totally in."

Girls with antlers
carry you from dawn to dusk.

They inflate the bellows.
Massage your neighborhood.

After the ether ponies have raced around
your sarcophagus,

after you've drunk enough potcheen
to earn Celtic blood,

after you've listened to "Danny Boy"
for the 10,000th time,

only then will girls with antlers
anoint your feet with margarine,

steep you in black tea
to dye your skin with tannins,

tie a raven to your wrist
so you may dance

nimbly across teacups.

Spirit House

The young Indian came into Meenehan's Hardware
every time they let him out of jail. He'd march in
the front door and walk to where he knew we kept
the sealants and glues. He'd buy a container and the
clerk would put it in a brown paper bag, and as we watched
he'd march across the street by Clyde's, squeeze into the
alley, open the container, and huff and huff from that
brown paper bag until he collapsed.

One day the police came in. Two young guys. Walkie Talkies
rattling off motion picture mumbo jumbo and static. And
they asked us not to sell any more glue to the guy. Said
he was a Nam vet who'd just never been able to cope with
coming back to the states.

I watched the owner's son throw him out once. But he just
waited until the next shift and finally found a clerk who'd
sell it to him.

And the Indian's life went on this way for how long I
don't know. He'd be out of jail and cleaned up for a couple
hours and then he'd buy the glue and huff it and they'd
find him passed out in the alley and drag him back
downtown. He'd be in the joint a week or two and then he'd
be released and it'd start all over.

This was back in the early 80's. Meenehan's lost their
lease soon after. Tough to imagine the guy lasting very
much longer. A bigger appetite for oblivion than any I've
ever seen.

Race Poem in Three Parts

DC 1973

I was picking up trash at this small park
near Fort Totten and a tiny kid asked me
"Why you want to be white?" Like I had a choice.

Phladelphia 2010

I'm at a reading and two 20-something
sistahs sit down beside me with an infant.
The little boy's asleep until mom removes
his hat and booties. He wakes slowly, blinks,
looks around, and his eyes settle on me.

His scream is so loud—a blood curdling
turn out the lights the party's over lamentation
I must have bumped my head on the ceiling
several times it was so unexpected.

I guess he didn't see many white people
in his day-to-day existence. He quiets down
eventually and before the reading is over
he's sneaking peeks at me—exotic
specimen that I am—a DC poet in Philly.

Eventually he tries to pull up on my legs,
tries to maintain his top-heavy balance.
"He likes your shirt," the young mom says.
And he sticks his perfect tiny palm
out and grabs a hold of my blue and white
Hawaiian shirt. His eyes glowing
in a eureka moment.

DC 1973

"I didn't ask to be born this way," I said.
Trying just as hard as this tiny kid
to understand differences.

Time Passages

If you live long enough
in the same town
you become a time machine

able to interpret layers of
cultural detritus and sediment,
to remember what came before
the here and now.

If you live long enough
in the same neighborhood
you become Homer

with many stories to tell
to an increasingly younger
and younger audience.

Who wouldn't relish this role?
Singer, historian, archaeologist,
storyteller, poet, sage, living
embodiment of an age.

My Washington DC is a series
of transparencies I continually
shuffle over top of the existing
superstructure.

My Washington DC is inhabited
by ghosts who jog in place
wondering when I will
crossover and join them.

VII

Utowana Lake, NY

Black hooded mushrooms
like bear scat along the trail.
Too numerous to avoid. Stinky
in the waffle of my boots.

At the waterfall I delight.
My sore feet in the frigid
mountain water. That rush
of sound revitalizing me. As though

all of the conversations
ever spoken were being said
in one explosive rush. As though
I might actually understand them.

Autumn Crocuses

sublime
where sun
spins to shadow

violet and white tapers
soften a hillside
curve

rusty
yellow
stamen

divine
yoga

Blue October

Ferns turn brown
a leitmotif
decaying
like cancerous lungs

Fallen apples
munched by deer
eyes shiny
in my flashlight

Bear scat
by the airplane hangar
a flock of turkeys
promenade the shore

Raindrops
drizzle stones
a dainty filigree
above the rackety creek

Eagle Lake, NY

After hiking nearly an hour,
a fork in the trail. Muddy lumber
track or a fallen birch block
your path.

Sunlight filters down
like dust mote days in a tiny apartment.
Voices from the lake. A motorboat.
All hidden from view.

You imagine bears in trees
gorging on apples, falling asleep
until awakened by your puny flashlight.

You imagine an Indian tribe
making their way back from a day
of bountiful fishing.

A crow protests above you.
Somewhere past the fallen birch.
You choose the mud.

Away from the lake shore
and deeper into the dark Huron forest.
Nobody knows where you are.
Nobody knows where you're going.

Memory Loss

The lake reflects tamarack and fir
a black jade adorned by water striders
rippled by a reticent breeze.

She sits in a moss green Adirondack chair
her brain nearly inundated.
Water over the dam.

Islands dot her landscape now.
Memories tucked into kayaks
and canoes that paddle in the distance.

Patagonia

Blue ice
Water everywhere

What exactly is magical realism?

Fish really do
swim through windows

Comfortable Lies

You've ringed your room with wildflowers:
bluish-green Purple Cliffbrake fern,
yellow bell-like flower of the Fawn Lily with mottled brown leaves,
Dutchman's Breeches that look like starched white trousers.

A wolf spider lives on the screen
by the propped open window.

What Could Be More Prehistoric Than Sex?

We drive to Broadkill Beach under a full moon
to watch the horseshoe crabs spawning run.

And I'm reminded of high school dances
where I stood alone until it was time to go home.

The all too familiar way males are gathered by the shoreline
smoking, trying to look hip,

comparing barnacles or the size of spiky tails,
cooling their jets until the females arrive.

And just like magic the much larger females appear
Mama Cass to these abbreviated Don Juans.

Big Mamas ostensibly taking no notice
of males colliding like bumper cars in their wake.

If horseshoe crabs could toss their ponytails…well,
you get the picture.

Dinky brown helmets jockey for position
hooking their way into a train of shells.

Females awkwardly crawl the beach looking every
bit like prehistoric spiders that refused to die.

Are they conscious of the males
hitchhiking on their backs?
This hits a raw nerve.
They ain't heavy they're my husbands.

Reminding me that every woman
is really Catherine Deneuve

at the end of *The Hunger*
buried up to her neck in old lovers.

I see gals complaining—
about guys, relationships, their exes.

Burrowing into the sand to lay their eggs
just like their mothers and their mother's mothers.

Ridiculous, inconsequential males,
fertilizing the eggs solo or in tandem.

Which leaves me flashing on single moms
and sunset encounters

at long ago Dewey Beach keggers.

Guys hanging around
like gold-chained Jersey gigolos.

Gals as perpetual motion dancing machines.

A new flotilla of helmets cresting on the high tide
like a preposterous D-Day re-enactment.

Yet what could be more beautiful
than genetic memory in action?

The continuation of the species.

Maybe there is something positive
to be said for this goofy process?

So many satellite males orbiting these
larger females that I can't move a step.

A symphony of clicking and digging,
the tide lapping on the beach.

Perhaps we can learn something from
this mad orgy of sex and sperm?

This dream world of horseshoe crabs
piled atop one another on the polygamous shoreline.

VIII

After Noah Sealed the Ark

Most went about their business
as the rain began in earnest.

Two of everything?
Noah was a lunatic.

People begin to worry after Day 1.
The skies black and alive with lightning.

By Day 3, many had climbed up
to perch on their rooftops.

Covered with blankets, tents,
babies crying, children frightened.

Did Noah really say, 40 days and
40 nights? How could it rain that long?

Those with boats jumped into them.
Families near mountains began to climb.

By Day 5 Voices could be heard praying for God to
make the rain stop, make it stop.

People trapped on their rooftops gestured
frantically to passing boats.

"Save us," they cried. "Save us." But hearts
hardened and people did not aid one another.

Day 7, houses came apart, disintegrating
in the rushing water. Hillsides washed away.

Screams were literally drowned out.
Bloated bodies floated everywhere.

By Day 8 people rowed to the Ark and hammered
on the wooden sides begging Noah to let them in.

On Day 9 the water was deep enough for the Ark's
supports to give way. Noah was afloat at last.

The crews of larger boats left their moorings.
They'd take their chances riding out the storm.

By Day 10 there was nary a building that hadn't been
washed away or covered over by the deluge.

So far so good on the mountain pathways.
People hiked a little higher each day.

By Day 15 the only land visible to the sailors
were the mountain tops they'd seen from afar.

The wind increased in strength
minute by minute. Nights were the worst.

Waves churning up the earth
smashed rubble into small boats.

People screamed as they capsized
and disappeared beneath the white caps.

By Day 20 the last survivors atop
what had once been mountains

now tiny islands in the roiling sea
had reached the summit with nowhere

left to go. Some cursed God,
others begged for God's forgiveness.

To the last they stretched
their arms toward heaven.

Pad Thai

The Filipina at the old-style
Oriental market says,

"Why don't you just go to a
Thai restaurant and buy some."

Missing the point entirely.

I want to master something new.
The rice noodles do what I want.

The sauce is my enemy.
Won't play ball. And then

I forget the onions and cilantro.

Still, in all it's not bad. I managed
the scrambled egg exactly right.

And the oil. The tofu is my friend
doing everything I ask. Though

crushing peanuts with a cup

is really plain laughable.
I need a mortar and pestle.

My cooking a kind of alchemy,
or medieval Zen therapy.

Like gardening. Like raking leaves.

The author at the 2010 Milton Poetry Festival
Photo by Shelley Grabel

ABOUT THE AUTHOR

RICHARD PEABODY is the founder and co-editor of *Gargoyle Magazine* and editor (or co-editor) of twenty-one anthologies including *Mondo Barbie*, *Conversations with Gore Vidal*, and *A Different Beat: Writings by Women of the Beat Generation*. The author of a novella, two short story collections, and six poetry books, he is also a native Washingtonian. Peabody teaches fiction writing at Johns Hopkins University, where he has been presented both the Faculty Award for Distinguished Professional Achievement (2005) and the Award for Teaching Excellence: Master of Arts in Writing Program (2010-2011).

Other Books from The Broadkill River Press

Sounding the Atlantic
Poetry by
Martin Galvin
ISBN 978-0-9826030-1-7
$14.95

That Deep & Steady Hum
Poetry by
Mary Ann Larkin
ISBN 978-0-9826030-2-4
$14.95

Exile at Sarzanna
Poetry by
Laura Brylawski-Miller
ISBN 978-0-9826030-5-5
$12.00

**The Year of the
Dog Throwers**
Poetry by
Sid Gold
ISBN 978-0-9826030-3-1
$12.00

Domain of the Lower Air
Fiction by
Maryanne Khan
ISBN 978-0-9826030-4-8
$14.95

Books from The Broadkill Press Chapbook Series

Loopholes
Poetry by
David P. Kozinski
**2009 Winner of the
Dogfish Head Poetry Prize**
ISBN 978-0-9826030-0-0
$7.00

Fractured Light
Poetry by
Amanda Newell
**2010 Winner of the
Dogfish Head Poetry Prize**
ISBN 978-0-9826030-7-9
$7.95

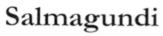

Salmagundi

Sherry Gage Chappelle

2011 Winner
Dogfish Head Poetry Prize

Salmagundi
Poetry by
Sherry Gage Chapelle
**2011 Winner of the
Dogfish Head Poetry Prize**
ISBN 978-0-9826030-9-3
$9.00

Constructing Fiction

Constructing Fiction
Advice on the Craft by
Jamie Brown
ISBN 978-0-9826030-8-6
$6.00

Jamie Brown

CPSIA information can be obtained at www.ICGtesting.com
Printed in the USA
BVOW070338060812

297054BV00001B/1/P